OPEN TO THE POWER OF THE CHAKRAS!

If you could effect a transformative change for the better in your life, would you? You can—by learning about the chakras as gateways to the divine energy within you.

The *Truth About Chakras* explains how knowledge and use of the ancient and powerful chakra system can bring enhanced physical health, emotional balance, personal power, love, creativity, and heightened perception and awareness. Learn simple exercises you can do to enhance your divine potential, and gain new keys to greater expression, personal freedom, and spiritual growth.

Discover for yourself the profound wisdom of this ancient Tantric system used by mystics for thousands of years.

A spiritual adventure awaits you!

About the Author

Anodea Judith is founder/director of LIFEWAYS in Northern California. As a professional healer and bodyworker, she has studied acupressure, yoga, bioenergetics, pshychic healing and reading, gestalt therapy, radical psychiatry, ritual magic, and shamanism. She serves as Priestess and President of the Church of All Worlds, helping run its subsidiary organizations, Forvever Forests, Nemeton, Ecosophical Research Assoc., and Holy Order of Mother Earth.

To Write to the Author

If you wish to contact the author or would like more information about this book, please write to the author in care of Llewellyn Worldwide and we will forward your request. Both the author and publisher appreciate hearing from you and learning of your enjoyment of this book and how it has helped you. Llewellyn Worldwide cannot guarantee that every letter written to the author can be answered, but all will be forwarded. Please write to:

Anodea Judith
c/o Llewellyn Worldwide
P.O. Box 64383, Dept. L362-0,
St. Paul, MN 55164-0383, U.S.A.

LLEWELLYN'S VANGUARD SERIES

The Truth About

CHAKRAS

by Anodea Judith

Author of
Wheels of Life

2000
Llewellyn Publications
P.O. Box 64383-362, St. Paul, MN 55164-0383
U.S.A.

For permissions, or for serialization, condensation, or for adaptations, write the Publisher.

First Edition
First Printing, 1990
Second Edition
Second Printing, 2000

International Standard Book Number:
0-87542-362-0

Illustrations: Anodea Judith
Chakra Lotuses: Geoffrey Ely

LLEWELLYN PUBLICATIONS
A Division of Llewellyn Worldwide, Ltd.
P.O. Box 64383 St. Paul, MN 55164-0383
www.llewellyn.com

Printed in the United States of America

Books by Anodea Judith

*Eastern Body, Western Mind: Psychology and the
Chakra System as a Path to the Self* (Celstial Arts)
*The Sevenfold Journey: Reclaiming Mind, Body, and
Spirit through the Chakras with Selene Vega*
     (Crossing Press)
Wheels of Life: A User's Guide to the Chakra System
(Llewellyn Publications)

Audiotape

Wheels of Life: A Journey Through the Chakras
     (Llewellyn Publications)

Llewellyn Publications is the oldest publisher of New
Age Sciences in the Western Hemisphere. This book is
one of a series of introductory explorations of each of the
many fascinating dimensions of New Age Science—each
important to a new understanding of Body and Soul,
Mind and Spirit, of Nature and humanity's place in the
world, and the vast unexplored regions of Microcosm
and Macrocosm.

Please write for a full list of publications.

THE SYSTEM OF CHAKRAS

A chakra is a *spinning vortex of energy* created within ourselves by the interpenetration of consciousness and the physical body. Through this combination, chakras become *centers of activity for the reception, assimilation and transmission of life energies.* Uniting the chakras is what we experience as the "self." It is through our chakras that our self grows and changes and interacts with the world.

The word *chakra* comes from the Sanskrit word for "wheel" or disk" and originated within the philosophy of the ancient yoga systems of India, most specifically from the Tantric texts. In this system, there are seven major chakras arranged vertically along the spine, starting at the base of the spine and ending at the top of the head (see Figure 1). In the physical body, these seven chakras correspond to major nerve ganglia, glands of the endocrine system, and various bodily processes, such as breathing, digesting, or procreating. While the chakras do exist *within* the physical body, exhibiting strong influence on such things as body shape or health, they are not made of any physical components themselves. A physician could not operate on a chakra anymore than an emotion, yet both can and do affect us physically.

Figure 1

In the psychological realm (by which I include the mental, emotional and spiritual), the chakras correspond to major areas of our lives, such as survival, sex, power, love, communication, perception, and understanding (see Table of Correspondences, Figure 2).

Taking the original meaning of the word chakra one step further, the chakras within us can be seen as our internal "floppy disks" that store our programming about how to function in life. The base chakra contains our survival program, such as what we like to eat and when we need exercise; the second chakra—our sexuality program, such as ethics and preferences; the upper chakras—our modes of perception and information storage. Our body is the computer hardware, and each of us has a slightly different model, programmed in a distinct language with unique operating systems. Ideally, one's work on the chakras is to examine the programming we have been given on each of these levels, eliminating destructive programming and consciously recreating something more beneficial.

Philosophically, the chakras correspond to major archetypal concepts, such as the elements of earth, water, fire, air, sound, light, and thought. The elements describe the essential nature of that chakra's function, such as earth that contains, water that flows, or fire that transforms. Numerous other correspondences, such as colors, sounds, herbs and gemstones, have also been correlated to the chakras and can be used as tools for accessing and developing them.

There are many smaller chakras throughout the body, such as those in our hands and feet. These are functioning centers like any of the others but are not usually attributed to major philosophical areas. Yet, those working with their hands are likely to have well-developed hand chakras, and a runner might have well-developed channels through their foot chakras.

As a composite system, the seven chakras describe a set of patterns that are evident through many aspects of life. In terms of cultural evolution, they describe the stages our race has been through and where we are going, from the first chakra survival consciousness of the Paleolithic era to the power-dominated (third chakra) consciousness of the present era.

In terms of individual development, the chakras describe the progression from infancy to early adulthood that repeats itself again from adulthood to old age as we establish our survival strategies, form sexual relationships, develop our personal power, communicate, vision, and learn. As we understand the significance of these levels, we can better develop appropriate strategies for coping with our situations, whether personal or cultural.

TABLE OF CORRESPONDENCES

CHAKRA	ONE	TWO	THREE	FOUR	FIVE	SIX	SEVEN
Sanskrit name	Muladhara	Svadhisthana	Manipura	Anahata	Visudaha	Ajna	Sahasrara
Location	Perineum	Lower Abdomen	Solar Plexus	Heart	Throat	Forehead	Top of Head
Element	Earth	Water	Fire	Air	Ether/Sound	Light	Thought
Psychological function	Survival, grounding	Emotions, sexuality	Will, power	Love, balance	Communication, creativity	Clairvoyance, imagination	Understanding, knowing
Emotion	Stillness	Desire, tears	Anger, joy, laughter	Love, compassion	Expansion, excitement	Dreaming	Bliss
Glands	Adrenals	Ovaries, prostate, testicles	Pancreas	Thymus	Hypothalamus, thyroid	Pineal	Pituitary
Other assoc. body parts	Legs, bones, large intestine	Womb, genitals, kidneys, bladder	Stomach, musculature	Lungs, heart, arms, hands	Throat, ears, mouth, arms, hands	Eyes	CNS, cerebral cortex
Malfunction	Obesity, hemorrhoids, constipation	Impotence, frigidity, uterine or bladder trouble	Ulcers, diabetes, hypoglycemia	Asthma, high blood pressure	Thyroid, colds, flu	Blindness, headaches, nightmares	Depression, alienation, confusion
# of petals	4	6	10	12	16	2	1000+
Color	Red	Orange	Yellow	Green	Blue	Indigo	Violet
Seed sound	Lam	Vam	Ram	Sam, yam	Ham	Om	ng-ng, as in sing
Vowel sound	o, as in rope	oo, as in due	uh, as in father	ay, as in play	ee, as in see	mmm, nnn	
Tarot suits	Pentacles	Cups	Wands	Swords			
Verb	I have	I feel	I can	I love	I speak	I see	I know
Qabala	Malkuth	Yesod	Hod, Netzach	Tiphareth	Geburah, Chesed	Binah, Chokmah	Kether
Planets	Earth, Saturn	Moon	Mars, Sun	Venus	Mercury, Neptune	Jupiter	Uranus
Animals	Elephant	Crocodile	Ram	Antelope	Deer	Owl	

Figure 2

Chakras are sometimes referred to as lotuses, for they open and close like a flower, and in the Tantric system they are shown with a varying number of petals. The petals, ranging from four at the base chakra to 1,000 or more at the crown, express their vibratory rate (see Table of Correspondences, Figure 2).

When a chakra is closed, the life force energy cannot travel through that part of the body, and one might say that the programming in that chakra is locked in a restrictive pattern. If this is the case, we feel a lack in our lives in its related area (such as the ability to communicate, chakra 5), and our physical health in the chakra's related functions may also be affected (sore throat, tight neck).

A chakra can also be "overblown" if it is out of balance with the other chakras in the system. In this case, that particular chakra uses so much of the body's energy and the mind's attention that other areas become deficient. An overblown third chakra causes an attachment to holding power over others hindering the ability to find the love and balance associated with the heart chakra directly above. As the chakras are discussed individually in the following pages, the results of a chakra that is too closed or too open will be examined more closely.

With attention and understanding, we can control and influence our chakras. They can be developed like muscles, programmed like a computer, nurtured like a seed, or closed like a book. Development of the chakras occurs through understanding the system as a whole and then working directly on specific areas. Techniques may include physical exercises, processing of old traumas through therapy, visualization and meditation, chanting of mantras, working with their elements, herbs, or gemstones, and personal ritual, as well as the general lessons that are brought to us through our daily lives.

The body is a vehicle of consciousness. The chakras can be seen as the wheels of life that carry this vehicle through its evolutionary journey toward enlightenment. Within us these wheels are like gears, each one appropriate for different activities or stages of life. As we open our chakras, we become more conscious and more fully alive. Our journey becomes smoother, more productive, yet more exciting as we become more fully who we are.

KUNDALINI

Kundalini is a concept often spoken of in relation to the chakras. Mythologically, Kundalini is a serpent Goddess who lies asleep at the base of the spine, coiled 3½ times around the first chakra, awaiting unfoldment. When she is awakened through any of a number of techniques, she unfolds and rises through the center of the body, piercing and awakening each chakra as she goes. When she has risen to the top or crown chakra, then all of the chakras have been opened, and a person is said to experience enlightenment.

Figure 3. The movement of energy created by gears connecting follows a snake-like path re- miniscent of Kundalini. When a chakra is too small, it cannot carry the charge on to the next chakra, and Kundalini's ascent stops.

What is this strange and mysterious Goddess force?

I like to think of Kundalini with a metaphor of connecting gears. In an undeveloped person, the chakras are likely to be small. Each one is spinning in its relative place, but the spinning of one does not necessarily affect the spinning of another. As the chakras grow through the capacity to handle increased energy, they are more likely to touch each other and thereby stimulate the spinning of a chakra above or below (see Figure 3). When this occurs, we feel an increased rush of energy and awareness throughout our whole system. We experience the Kundalini force.

Kundalini is a strong and powerful force which can produce radical physical and mental changes. Some find it hard to function in the day-to-day world when the Kundalini force is strong. Others find it an exhilarating and enlightening experience. Some say it is sublimated sexual energy; others say it is vibrational rhythm entrainment between brain waves and physiological subsystems. There are many theories and none of them are conclusive. It can be triggered by yoga practices, meditation, physical stimulation (such as a car accident or strenuous exercise), mental excitement (scary movies sometimes do it to me) or by a learned master in the art of Kundalini awakening. It is generally *not* advisable to invoke Kundalini without a teacher or support system that can help you process the changes it may bring. It is, however, a *healing force*, and is most beneficial to us when we can surrender to it gracefully.

Opening The Hand Chakras

To experience what a chakra feels like, try the following exercise.

Sit comfortably with your hands pushed straight out in front of you, elbows straight. Turn one palm downward and one palm up. Quickly, with repeated motions, open and close your fists tightly, as fast and for as long as you comfortably can. Switch the positions of your palms and repeat until your hands are tired.

Drop your arms, open your fists and bring your palms together *slowly*, moving them together and out again. Do you feel a ball of energy between your hands? If you tune in closely, you can feel the spinning. These are your hand chakras, a smaller version of your spinal chakras.

MULADHARA—THE ROOT CHAKRA

Element: Earth
Color: Red
Verb: I have
Attributes: Survival, grounding, solidity, the body

The first chakra is found at the base of the spine, the point you are sitting on right now. Its name, *Muladhara*, means "root," and the paths of energy in this chakra extend downward like a root through the legs and feet to contact the solid Earth below (see Figure 4).

Its color is a deep red, and its symbol is a lotus of four petals within which is a downward-pointing triangle, symbolizing the root energy.

A simple way to ener-gize this chakra is to sit up straight in your chair with your feet flat against the floor and push slightly into your feet. Your legs will tighten a bit and there will be an increased flow into your base chakra. As you relax your legs and feet, you will feel that flow recede, and as you tighten them, you can feel your body become more solid. It

Figure 4

is not necessary to push into our legs at all times for the first chakra to function, but this is a simple way we can increase the flow of energy into our lower body while doing such mental tasks as working at a desk, talking on the phone, watching TV, or sitting in a job interview.

The Muladhara chakra is the *foundation* for the whole chakra system. Its function is to respond to any issues concerning *survival*: eating, sleeping, exercising, recovering from illness, making a living, or simply feeling safe and secure. If our survival needs are properly taken care of, then we can safely focus on other levels, such as learning, creativity, or relationships. If there is some damage to the chakra, then we find ourselves repeatedly coping with threats to our survival, which keeps us from accomplishing other things. These threats might be changing jobs, having to move, recurrent health problems, weight problems, and/or a general feeling of fear for one's safety.

These are all issues that occur occasionally in the normal course of one's life. Anytime they occur, they trigger our first chakra programming. Having to move may make us feel insecure, bring on a cold, or make us eat more. It is only when such issues become a *frequent pattern* that a first chakra problem is indicated.

Survival consciousness is the primary state of the infant, and if this phase of life is properly taken care of, it should not be a recurrent issue later in life. Children who are abandoned, separated from their mothers at birth (such as incubator babies), physically abused, or suffering from severe childhood illnesses will be more likely to have first chakra problems throughout their lives.

The result can be the situational problems mentioned above, as well as psychological problems having to do with lack of focus or discipline, dependency on others, (unable to stand on one's own two feet), possible eating disorders, feeling vague and "spacy," and a general inability to "let down and relax." These are all signs that the first chakra is blocked in some way, generally indicating that the chakra does not open properly and allow the energy to flow through freely.

If, on the other hand, the chakra is too open, then we become overly attached at this level. We may be obsessed with money and possessions or our health, unable to allow change or to let go, and as a result we get stuck in the same routines, same old job, same old patterns.

When the chakra is closed, we lack stability. When it is too open, we are frozen solid. The ideal state would be to have stability *and* flexibility in balance.

The element associated with the first chakra is earth. Earth is solid, earth is heavy, earth is below us, and earth supplies us with our survival needs: food, clothing and shelter.

The universal force that flows downward, like roots, toward the Earth is gravity. Gravity is created by mass—the more mass something has, the stronger its gravity.

The force of gravity allows us to stay connected with the Earth. We need not *do* anything but relax, and gravity is there. When we allow ourselves to flow gracefully with gravity, we are in harmony with the downward flow of the first chakra.

The common term for this flow as it occurs in the human body is *grounding*. Grounding is a process of dynamic contact with the Earth that occurs through our legs and feet. When grounding is done appropriately, our whole body is nourished and energized.

Grounding is the building of a foundation. We ground ourselves in biology and chemistry before practicing medicine. We build a foundation before we build the walls of a house. Without a good foundation, nothing that follows will be as durable.

Grounding puts us in touch with our bodies. Uncovering the truths buried within our bodies brings us to a solid connection with our ground, manifesting in greater health, prosperity, and well-being.

Eating is a basic first chakra survival activity. Without food, we do not survive very long. Eating disorders (too much or too little) often indicate first chakra imbalance. Eating is a grounding activity—it helps to bring us down, helps us to feel settled, calm, secure. Excess weight can be an attempt to ground out high stress, to protect the body, or to replace proper grounding techniques. Eating too little or being chronically underweight can be an attempt to avoid grounding and physicality because it seems too frightening or confining.

Grounding Exercise

Stand upright with your feet shoulder-width apart, toes slightly in. (Take your shoes off so you can feel the floor under you.) Press into your feet as if you were trying to push the floorboards apart between your feet. You will feel a solidity come into your legs as you do this. This comes from pushing down into your feet.

Once you can feel that solidity, you are ready to begin the exercise. Inhale deeply and bend your knees, letting your belly relax. Now exhale and push into your feet s-l-o-w-l-y, pushing as you did before and allowing your legs to slowly straighten. Do not let them straighten all the way, but bend them again and inhale as you go down into your legs. Push again against the floor as you exhale, pushing your energy downward through your body.

Do not completely straighten your legs, keep breathing, and move slowly. If you are doing this correctly, you will start to feel a slow vibration in your legs as you push against the floor. This vibration is the charge of energy moving through your legs and into your first chakra. It can be used to push out blocks, to increase your sense of contact with your body, or to simply make you feel awake and refreshed.

It is possible to get overcharged, however, so exercise caution in how long you keep this up. If you get overcharged and feel anxious, kick your feet into a pile of pillows, shake your body, or let out whatever feelings are arising.

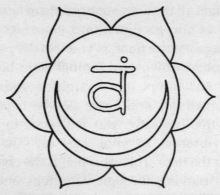

SVADHISTHANA—THE SEAT OF LIFE

Element: Water
Color: Orange
Verb: I feel, I want
Attributes: Polarity, movement, sexuality, pleasure, emotion

We have come from the Earth, energy that is still, solid, dense. We have gained an understanding of our bodies, our grounding, and things associated with one. We are now ready to introduce a new dimension.

As we enter the second chakra, we encounter *change*.

Our singleness becomes duality; our point becomes a line; the solid, a liquid; stillness becomes movement. We have gained a degree of freedom.

Through change we create and discover difference. Difference, at its extremes, creates polarities. Polarities create attraction and movement. Movement is essential and characteristic of all life.

The second chakra is in the lower abdomen, centered between the navel and the genitals. It corresponds to the sacral vertebrae and the nerve ganglion called the sacral plexus. This plexus hooks into the sciatic nerve and is a center of motion for the body. It is often called the "seat of life."

Its element is water. Therefore, the chakra corresponds with bodily functions having to do with liquid: circulation, urinary elimination, sexuality and reproduction.

Classically, this chakra is the center of sexuality, emotions, sensation, pleasure, movement, and nurturance. Like water, it is ruled by the Moon, which influences the tides and our emotions.

The Sanskrit name for the second chakra is *Svadhisthana*, which means "sweetness." This is an apt name for the sweetness of desire, pleasure, and sexuality associated with the life-giving waters of Svadhisthana. Its color is orange, and its lotus contains a crescent Moon surrounded by six petals.

The second chakra embodies the nature of "two" and runs on polarity, instigating the movement in the body and psyche that begins the climbing process of coiled Kundalini as she rises through the chakras. Encountering "other" creates desire, and desire gets us to move, to reach out, to grow and change.

All the chakras are connected by a non-physical channel running straight up the spine called the *sushumna*. Two alternate channels, *ida* and *pingala*, twist in figure-eight like patterns around each chakra, crossing the sushumna. These channels are among thousands of psychic channels called *nadis* (from *nad*, meaning "motion"). *Ida* and *pingala* represent the lunar and solar aspects, respectively. They are responsible for "charging" the chakras, causing them to spin (see Figure 5).

We have added a degree of consciousness to our bodily awareness. Our psychic sense at this level is experienced in the form of emotions. We may "feel" something is wrong, but the information is not yet conscious.

If the chakra is too open, there is a tendency to feel everyone else's emotions or to be overly ruled by one's own emotions with frequent and dramatic emotional episodes. If the chakra is closed down, then we are flat, dull, lifeless, dry. We are out of touch with our emotions, have very little desire or passion, and little or no interest in sexuality.

Ideally, we should be able to embrace polarities, feel our emotions, and express ourselves sexually without losing the connection with our own center.

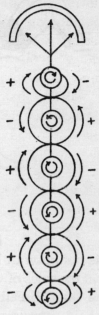

Figure 5

The main aspect of the second chakra, however, is *sexuality*. Sexuality is a life force. It is the water that softens the hard Earth and readies it for change. It is a force too often denied or perverted, and being robbed of our pleasure, we are robbed of our power. When we lose our desire, we lose our will. Power and will are attributes of the next chakra, and pleasure and desire are their seed. Sexuality is the flower of that seed. Power and will are its fruits.

Figure 6

EXERCISE
Pelvic Rock 1

Lie flat on your back with your knees bent so that the soles of your feet are planted firmly on the floor. Breathe into your chest fully and exhale completely, pushing into your feet at the end of the exhale and tipping your pelvis upward. Imagine you are pushing the breath out between your legs.

When the exhale is spent, relax your legs and hips, returning them to the floor, and inhale fully into your chest again. Then repeat. Keep this going for a minimum of five minutes to feel the effects.

Pelvic Rock 2

If the first one stirs up a great deal of energy, or if there is too much stiffness to perform it smoothly, try repeating the same sequence much faster. In this exercise the pelvis is snapped up and back quickly, with as much force as possible. Let yourself make any sounds that are natural. This helps to release blocked energy. (Make sure you do this on something soft like a mat or bed.)

MANIPURA—THE POWER CHAKRA

Element: Fire
Color: Yellow
Verb: I can
Attributes: Power, will, energy, transformation

Earth, water, fire. With our bodies grounded and our emotions flowing, we now move on to power, energy and will.

This is our third chakra, a yellow lotus of ten petals, located .at the solar plexus—the place where we get those butterfly feelings when we feel scared or powerless. Its element is fire—fire—that radiates and transforms matter into energy, giving light and warmth. This chakra represents our "get up and go," our action, our will, our vitality, and our sense of personal power. Its name, *Manipura*, means "lustrous gem." We can think of it as a glowing yellow Sun, radiating through the center of our body.

On the physical plane, the third chakra rules metabolism, the process whereby we turn food (matter) into energy and action.

Digestion troubles, stomach troubles, hypoglycemia, diabetes, ulcers, or addictions to stimulants, such as caffeine, are all related to malfunctioning of the third chakra. Weight problems may also be an indication that the body is not properly turning its matter into energy.

We can also assess the health of this chakra by examining our body structure at this level: tight, hard stomachs, sunken diaphragms, or large potbellies are all indications of third chakra excess or deficiency.

Examining your relationship to the properties of fire can give further clues to the nature of your third chakra. Are you frequently cold, physically or emotionally? Do you get overheated, hot-tempered? Is your style quick and energetic, or slow and lethargic?

When the third chakra is closed down, one may feel tired, afraid, shaky, quiet, or withdrawn. There is a fear of taking risks, confronting people or issues, taking charge, and with all this, a lack of energy. There may be too much seriousness and not enough laughter, ease or fun, all of which help the third chakra open and relax. Pleasure, from the chakra below, helps make the fire warm and easy; without it, our fires are cold and hard.

If the chakra is too open, then we have a kind of bully archetype—someone who also needs to be in control, to dominate, to seek after power, prestige, ambition. As the lower chakras in general are more ego-oriented, third chakra excess can make a person narcissistically self-centered.

An appropriate concept for a healthy balance in this chakra is the archetype of the warrior—standing strong, staying in touch with feelings, confronting only when appropriate and quietly maintaining a sense of power. A healthy third chakra can take on a task and complete it, take on a risk and not be bound by perfectionism, or act in the role of leadership without domination or self-aggrandizement.

In the second chakra we encountered desire. Desire is the fuel for the will, the passion within our body giving strength to decisions made by the mind. Fire is the spark of life that ignites will to action. Fire is the spark that lies between the poles, and the third chakra creates power by combining the polarity introduced by the second chakra, just as electricity is made by the combination of polarities. Having made yet another step toward consciousness, we now temper our desires and instincts with knowledge, making decisions that are then put into action, again combining the poles of mind and body.

Power, then, is seen as an act of combination, of joining together parts to make a greater whole. When we embrace and combine all the parts within us—our bodies, our emotions, our visions, our knowledge—then we emerge whole and powerful.

A good rule of thumb for stimulating the third chakra is to get your energy moving. Jogging, yelling, or pounding a pillow can help you loosen up. Or you might try the following exercise.

Figure 7

EXERCISE
Woodchopper

Stand with feet planted firmly on the ground, knees slightly bent, heels about two feet apart. Raise arms together over the head with hands joined. Arch back slightly. Making an "ah" sound as you descend, swing the whole upper portion of the body downward bringing your hands between your legs and through. The motion should be smooth and rapid, emitting as much force and power as is possible. Let the sound be full and loud. Repeat five to ten times in a session, and feel the energy break through into your upper body. This exercise is also an excellent anger release.

ANAHATA—THE HEART CHAKRA

Element: Air
Color: Green
Verb: I love
Attributes: Love, balance, relationship, compassion

We are now halfway through our seven-leveled chakra system. Below us are the first three chakras which relate to things and activities in the external physical world. Above us are the top three chakras which relate to internal representations of the physical world that are experienced mentally. The fourth chakra, located over the heart, is the balance point between these two extremes: the integrator of mind and body, believed to be the central home of the spirit.

The 12-petaled lotus symbol of the heart chakra contains within it two intersecting triangles forming a six-pointed star. These triangles represent the force of matter moving upward toward liberation and the force of spirit moving into manifestation. It is at this chakra that they are evenly combined, creating a center of peace and balance. Its seed sound is "yam" and its animal is an antelope, running free.

The heart chakra is related to the element air and the quality of love. Air is formless, largely invisible, absolutely necessary, and the least dense of our first four elements. Air is expansive as it will expand to fit any space it is put into, yet it is soft and gentle.

So, too, is love. Love is the expansion of the heart, the transcendence of boundaries, the interconnectedness of spirit. Love is balance, ease, softness, forgiveness. And love at the heart chakra is felt as a state of being, existing independently of any object or person, unlike the passion-oriented love of the second chakra.

The Sanskrit name for this chakra is Anahata, which means "sound that is made without any two things striking." This describes a state where we are no longer fighting or confronting what we love but moving with it in graceful harmony. The fight of the third chakra gives way to graceful acceptance in the fourth.

Because Anahata is related to the element air, it is accessible through the breath. The Hindus call the breath prana, which means "first unit," and they believe it contains the essence of all vitality and nourishment, being the point of commonality between the mental and physical worlds. Opening up the breath, unloosening whatever tensions are constricting it, is a way of accessing the heart chakra.

If the heart chakra is closed down, the very core of us suffers. Our breathing is shallow, slowing down our metabolism and our physical energy. Blocked at the center, we feel divided between mind and body. We pull in to ourselves, withdraw, and become a closed system.

When the heart chakra is too open, there is a tendency to give all our time and energy away, to be so focused on "other" that we lose our own center.

Ideally, the heart chakra should radiate love from a strong, solid center of self-acceptance and reach out with supportive care and compassion toward others. With its essential message of balance, our self-love and love for others need to be balanced and interconnected. Directly below the heart chakra is another small lotus that is seldom talked about but significant to the heart chakra. Called the *Anandakanda lotus*, it has eight petals and contains the *Kalpataru*, or the Celestial Wishing Tree. In front of the tree is an altar for worship, and it is believed that the tree contains the deeper wishes of the heart chakra—those things we hardly dare name but are most integral to our deepest hopes. It is believed that when one worships at this altar by wishing from the heart, the tree bestows even more than is desired.

The operating force in this chakra is the force of *equilibrium*. That which stays in balance has longevity and lives in harmony. Enter the peaceful balance of the heart within yourself and others, and you will experience the mysteries of Anahata.

EXCERCISE
The Arch

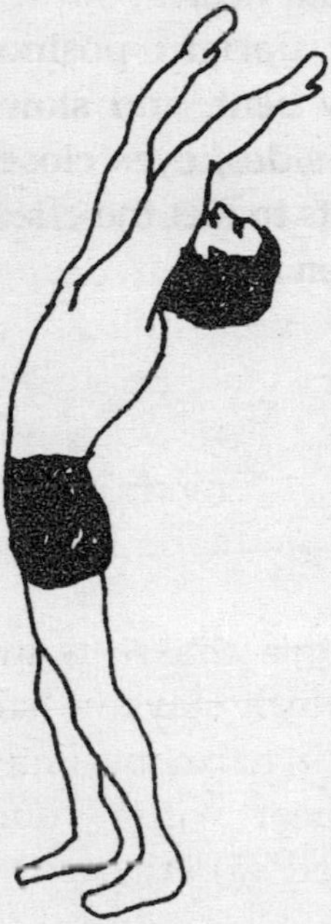

Form the grounding position of chakra one and begin breathing into your legs, building up some charge." Then bring the charge into your pelvis by moving your hips back and forth until your second chakra feels some of this same energy.

When your hips and belly feel connected, begin to form an arch with your body, keeping your knees bent, thrusting your pelvis forward, then your stomach and chest, and finally reaching upward with your arms, head back. (Be gentle with your spine, and do *not* hold this position if you start to feel any discomfort.)

Figure 8

If you are holding the position correctly, you should feel a vibration in your chest. Breathe into this and relax as much as you can in this difficult position, imagining a green light filling and opening your heart.

Return *slowly* to your upright position, keeping the knees slightly bent, and slowly return your arms to your sides, eyes closed. Stand at rest a few moments to feel the effects of this exercise. Repeat when ready.

VISUDDHA—THE THROAT CHAKRA

Element: Sound
Color: Bright Blue
Verb: I speak
Attributes: Sound, vibration, communication, creativity

Chakra 5 is located in the region of the neck and shoulders and is the center of *communication and creativity*. Its color is a bright turquoise blue, mixing the deep indigo of the sixth chakra with the green of the heart. Its lotus has 16 petals, upon which are inscribed all the vowels of the Sanskrit language. Vowels are generally thought to represent spirit, while consonants give the edges and definitions which define matter. As we enter chakra 5, we are crossing deeper into the realms of mind and spirit.

This lotus is called *Visuddha*, which means "purification." To successfully reach and open the fifth chakra, the body must attain a certain level of purification, which helps to achieve the sensitivity needed for the subtler levels of the upper chakra.

Classically, the element associated with this level is ether, or *akasha*, meaning "spirit," as well as the element of sound. Sound is a rhythmic vibration of air molecules as they are impacted by matter in movement. If I clap my hands, the sound that reaches you is from the air I have displaced. All sound is a vibration, and all things, living and nonliving, have a unique vibration. At this level, we do not see the world as individual things or their activities but as a complex interwoven net of energies with characteristic vibrational rhythms.

The Hindus believe that the universe itself is made of sound. Mother Kali, the destroyer, is said to have the power to remove the letters of the alphabet from the petals of the chakras when she chooses to destroy the world. Without sound and language, there is no form.

Sound waves are subject to a principle called *resonance*, also known as "rhythm entrainment" or "sympathetic vibration." Resonance is what occurs when sound waves of similar frequency meet—they lock into phase, with their vibrations oscillating at the same time. That which is in phase tends to remain in phase; hence, the interlocking of vibrational waves creates the ongoing harmony and substance that we experience in the world. Our breathing, heart rate, brain waves, and sleeping and eating patterns are all rhythmic activities that "entrain" or connect us with the world around us. When we are feeling harmonious with our surroundings, then our internal rhythms are resonating within ourselves. This resonance will, in turn, call other wave forms into harmony with it, bringing strength and integrity to the organism.

From sound we get communication. Communication is the activity and function of the fifth chakra. Here we have language, a complex pattern of sound and rhythm, through which we symbolize the physical world around us. Through symbol, we have a more efficient way of dealing with the world. I can describe my car, but I can't bring it into the room with me. I can call New York without actually going there. Our minds work with symbols. We think in words, as well as image and sensory memory. The world of the upper chakras is symbolic of the world below.

Communication is a rhythmic activity. The more resonant our own internal rhythms, the more easily and pleasantly we will communicate. Studies have shown that regardless of the content of words used, listeners and speakers enter into a rhythm entrainment as they converse. It is believed that understanding occurs only when entrainment can take place.

Communication involves both listening and speaking. If one's fifth chakra is closed down, then there is fear of expressing oneself, fear of speaking one's truth, or excessive shyness. The voice itself is timid and the words are few. If the chakra is too open, we are so busy expressing that we forget to listen or our voice is dissonant, and we are unable to enter into resonance with those around us.

Ideally, the fifth chakra should be connected to the self—to all the other chakras above and below—to visions of the mind and the feelings from body with equal ease.

Chanting is an activity that increases the overall resonance of our being, allowing all our internal systems to enter into a rhythmic harmony. When chanting is practiced as a group activity, it enhances resonance and communication with the group as a whole. From Zen monasteries to rock concerts, this is a powerful tool for enhancing collective consciousness.

The fifth chakra is also a center of creativity, another form of symbolic communication. As we open up this center, we open up our creative potential. The greater our resonance within, the greater the power within our creations.

Experiment with the resonant frequency of your chakras by chanting the following tones with each chakra, varying the pitch from low to higher as you climb up the chakras. Try to find the pitch that resonates with your body. Work on letting your sound be full-bodied and resonant.

Chakra One: Ooo as in home
Chakra Two: U as in rule
Chakra Three: Ah as in father
Chakra Four: Ay as in play
Chakra Five: Ee as in free
Chakra Six: Mm as in hum
Chakra Seven: Ng as in sing

AJNA—THE VISION CENTER

Element: Light
Color: Indigo
Verb: I see
Attributes: Clairvoyance, memory, dreams, vision, color

Chakra 6, located at the level of the forehead, is also known as the third eye. A lotus with only two petals, it is visualized as a deep indigo blue. This is the center of visual, psychic and intuitive perception—the place where we store our memories, perceive our dreams, and imagine our future.

Its name, *Ajna*, means both "to perceive" and "to command." Just as words are used to shape our world, so do the images we hold in our minds influence the events of our lives. What we perceive and remember is also what we command. A visualization held strongly is the first step in bringing an ethereal thought-form into manifestation.

Its element is light, a higher, faster vibration than that of sound, the least dense and most versatile of any element we have encountered thus far. Traveling at speeds beyond comprehension, communicating across distances events that may have ceased to exist millenia ago, light in all its splendor allows us to perceive the world in an infinite display of pattern. And when we view the world, we must remember that it is not objects we see but reflected light.

The Ajna chakra relates to the *pineal gland*, a vestigial light sensitive organ located in the exact geometric center of the head. In the embryo, the pineal begins as an actual third eye and later degenerates. It has been demonstrated that the pineal gland is sensitive to light, even when optical nerves have been cut. However, the functioning of the pineal in the mature adult is still a mystery. It is believed by some to play a part in producing the internal visions that sometimes come with meditative states.

Chakra 6 is our *intuitive* level, bringing us information through internally experienced visual imagery. Dreams are the clearest example of this. Clairvoyant sight is the ultimate example—the product of an open and functioning Ajna chakra. The purpose of this center is to become aware of the images inside our minds—the ones we perceive and the ones we create—so that this vast visual screen can be used consciously to call images at will and bring us information unavailable through other means.

Those who are open on this level are aware of their perceptions and can interpret them usefully. If the chakra is closed down, we may experience eye trouble, headaches, or troubling dreams. If the chakra is too open without solid ground to back it up, one may experience hallucinations, confusion from too much input, or over-interpretation of everyday occurrences.

It is my firm belief that psychic perception is something that everyone has and uses profusely, whether or not they are aware of it. It is important to validate these subtle psychic perceptions that float through our minds each day.

Opening psychic perception is largely a function of learning to recognize patterns and creating an internal visual language with which to interpret them. If you see someone has done something in the past, chances are likely it will happen again. As we climb higher into the upper chakras, we approach a sense of divine order, and perception of that order allows us easily and accurately to "fill in the blanks" and perceive, like light waves, that which is actually at a distance, spatially and temporally.

Outside of our own imaginations, the images that surround and rule us are a major factor in mass consciousness. Television, billboards, clothing trends, cinematography and other visual media feed into our consciousness on an immediate and whole brain level. To clear the chakra, we must get away from the images of what we expect to see and begin to experience the world with the freshness of a child. Only then can our organ of psychic perception begin to see accurately. And when we do, we discover an exciting world of patterns and colors unlike anything in the physical realm.

Each of the chakras is related to a color, and though the system has changed from the ancient Tantrics to modern associations, the most popular pattern is the *rainbow spectrum*. Red light has the longest and slowest wavelength, so it is associated with chakra 1, and the chakras proceed in rainbow order to the violet at the crown.

A good exercise to develop the visualization capacity of your third eye, while simultaneously helping to balance all your chakras, is to focus on each one of your chakras, filling that part of your body with the appropriate color of light. Begin at the top or the bottom, but proceed in order, and take time with each chakra to fully feel the effects.

Chakra One: Red
Chakra Two: Orange
Chakra Three: Yellow
Chakra Four: Green
Chakra Five: Bright Blue
Chakra Six: Indigo
Chakra Seven: Violet

SAHASRARA—THE CROWN

Element: Thought
Color: Violet
Verb: I know
Attributes: Information, understanding, awareness, consciousness, pattern, meditation

At last we come to the end of our journey, climbing to the nectar blossom of our flower— the thousand-petaled lotus sitting at the crown of the head. This is the chakra of *thought, consciousness*, and *information*, our most abstract and versatile level of all the chakras. Like the Muladhara, which has its roots in matter, the Sahasrara chakra, which means "thousand-fold" has its thousand petals of spirit reaching into the infinite cosmos. To the Hindus, thousand is a way of expressing infinity, and indeed, this chakra has no limits in its scope.

The element of Sahasrara is thought, a fundamentally distinct and unmeasurable entity that is the first and barest manifestation of the greater field of consciousness around us. Correspondingly, the function of the chakra is *knowing*, just as other chakras relate to seeing, doing, or feeling. It is through the crown chakra that we store and retrieve information and run it through our lower chakras to bring things into manifestation.

The crown chakra is most significantly characterized by a quality of "withinness," contrasting the external manifestation in time and space of the lower chakras. A single human brain contains some 13 billion interconnected nerve cells, capable of making more connections among themselves than the number of atoms in the universe. This staggering comparison leaves us with a pretty remarkable instrument. As there are 100 million sensory receptors in the body, and 10 trillion synapses in the nervous system, we find that the mind is 100,000 times more sensitive to the organism's internal environment than the external. It is truly from a place within that we acquire and process our knowledge.

Withinness is a way of accessing a dimension that has no locality in time and space. If we postulate that each chakra represents a dimension of smaller and faster vibration, we theoretically reach a place in the crown chakra where we have a wave of infinite speed and no wavelength, allowing it to be everywhere at once and yet having no perceivable location. Ultimate states of consciousness are described as omnipresent. By reducing the world to a pattern system, occupying no physical dimension, we have infinite storage capacity for its symbols. In other words, we carry the whole world inside our heads.

Pattern implies order. To the Hindus, order is the one underlying universal reality, and that order is considered synonymous with consciousness. Consciousness, then, is a field of *ordered pattern*. Chakra 7 is our gateway to "cosmic consciousness" or "higher consciousness." These terms merely refer to awareness of a deeper, more encompassing order. It is the perception of meta-patterns, deep central truths about our cosmic ordering system. Manifesting our thought-forms into reality is a matter of following the lines of order we perceive.

The crown chakra is the place where we study consciousness itself, even though each chakra reflects a state of consciousness. It must be remembered in this study that what we are looking for is the very thing that is doing the looking. Intelligence is less a matter of finding the answers than of realizing who and what are asking the questions.

Thought is comprised of bits of information that we spend time organizing. Through our experiences, each one of us builds a personal matrix of information within our mind. From the first glimpses of our mother's face to our doctoral dissertation, we spend our time trying to put information about our world into some semblance of order. The very act of thinking is the process of following lines of order. Our matrix structures become our personal belief systems and the ordering principles of our lives. Not only do we organize new information into our personal structure, but we also order the events of our lives that bring us that information.

Kundalini is the "force" of consciousness. As she rises and descends, she changes the internal order of the personal matrix, each time allowing a greater perception of the whole. Each of the chakras represents a level of organization, valid for the work on its particular level. Each time Kundalini rises, we find ourselves needing to reorganize our lives to match the higher order She brings us.

While each chakra is a disk, programmed with information relating to its particular function, the seventh chakra can be seen as the overall operating system for the whole biocomputer. It represents our belief systems, the way we categorize our information, and even our ability to be aware at all. Thoughts are things, and they are the seeds from which all manifestation grows. Like all seeds, they contain the pattern that shapes the flower as it grows.

Following one's thoughts

Lie or sit in a comfortable meditation position. Allow your mind to become relatively calm and quiet, using whatever technique is most effective for you.

Gradually let yourself pay attention to the thoughts that pass through your mind. Pick one and ask yourself where it came from—what thoughts preceded it. Then follow to the origin of that thought. It may be something that occurred years ago or something that is pressing on you right now. Then again follow that thought to its source and on to each thought's origin. Eventually, we come to a kind of infinite source that has no objective origin.

Return and pick another thought that passes through. Repeat the same sequence, going further and further back. See how many of your thoughts emanate from a similar source—either an issue you're working with in your life right now, a past teaching, or your own place of connection with the infinite.

Conclusion

Together, the seven chakras form a connecting ladder between matter and consciousness, body and mind, Earth and Heaven. Each of us forms this ladder as the steps are found within us.

In order for us to be whole, the ladder must be complete. Therefore, each chakra is of equal importance, and the blocking of one chakra can make an excess or deficiency in another part of the system.

Individually, the chakras can give us important clues about our strengths and weaknesses, outlining areas in which we need to work on ourselves. It must be remembered, however, that the chakras form a *complete system*, and diagnosis or attention to any one area should always be seen in relation to the whole.

With our chakras opened and fully functioning, we ourselves form the rainbow bridge between Heaven and Earth, ever evolving towards realization and integration.

Wheels of Life
A User's Guide to the Chakra System
ANODEA JUDITH

An instruction manual for owning and operating the inner gears that run the machinery of our lives. Written in a practical, down-to-earth style, this fully illustrated book will take the reader on a journey through aspects of consciousness, from the bodily instincts of survival to the processing of deep thoughts.

Discover this ancient metaphysical system under the new light of popular Western metaphors: quantum physics, elemental magick, Kabbalah, physical exercises, poetic meditations, and visionary art. Learn how to open these centers in yourself, and see how the chakras shed light on the present world crises we face today. And learn what you can do about it!

This book will be a vital resource for: Magicians, Witches, Pagans, Mystics, Yoga Practitioners, Martial Arts people, Psychologists, Medical people, and all those who are concerned with holistic growth techniques.

0-87542-320-5
528 pp., 6 x 9, illus., softcover   **$17.95**

Chakras for Beginners

A Guide to Balancing Your Chakra Energies

DAVID POND

The chakras are spinning vortexes of energy located just in front of your spine and positioned from the tailbone to the crown of the head. They are a map of your inner world—your relationship to yourself and how you experience energy. They are also the batteries for the various levels of your life energy. The freedom with which energy can flow back and forth between you and the universe correlates directly to your total health and well-being.

Blocks or restrictions in this energy flow expresses itself as disease, discomfort, lack of energy, fear, or an emotional imbalance. By acquainting yourself with the chakra system, how they work and how they should operate optimally, you can perceive your own blocks and restrictions and develop guidelines for relieving entanglements.

With *Chakras for Beginners* you will discover what is causing any imbalances, how to bring your energies back into alignment, and how to achieve higher levels of consciousness.

1-56718-537-1
5 3/16 x 8, 216 pp., softcover $9.95

To order, call 1-800-THE MOON
Prices subject to change without notice

New Chakra Healing
The Revolutionary 32-Center Energy System
CYNDI DALE

Break through the barriers that keep you from your true purpose with New Chakra Healing. This manual presents never-before-published information that makes a quantum leap in the current knowledge of the human energy centers, fields, and principles that govern the connection between the physical and spiritual realms.

By working with your full energy body, you can heal all resistance to living a successful life. The traditional seven-chakra system was just the beginning of our understanding of the holistic human. Now Cyndi Dale's research uncovers a total of 32 energy centers: 12 physically oriented chakras, and 20 energy points that exist in the spiritual plane. She also discusses auras, rays, kundalini, mana energy, karma, dharma, and cords (energetic connections between people that serve as relationship contacts).

1-56718-200-3
304 pp., 7 x 10, illus., softcover $19.95

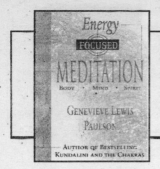

Energy Focused Meditation
Body, Mind, Spirit
GENEVIEVE PAULSON

Formerly titled Meditation & Human Growth.
Meditation has many purposes: healing, past life awareness, balance, mental clarity, and relaxation. It is a way of opening into areas that are beyond your normal thinking patterns. In fact, what we now call "altered states" and "peak experiences"— tremendous experiences of transcendental states— can become normal occurrences when you know how to contact the higher energy vibrations.

Most people think that peak experiences happen, at best, only a few times in life. Through meditation, however, it is possible to develop your higher awareness so you can bring more peak happenings about by concentrated effort. Energy Focused Meditation is full of techniques for those who wish to claim those higher vibrations and expanded awareness for their lives today.

1-56718-512-6
6 x 9, 224 pp., 17 illus. $12.95

Wheels of Life
A Journey Through the Chakras
ANODEA JUDITH

Anodea Judith, author of the best-selling book *Wheels of Life*, takes you on a journey through the power centers of the body: the chakras. Evocative music and powerful narration bring the listener to a new awareness of self.

0-87542-321-3
90 minutes   **$9.95**

To order, call 1-800-THE MOON
Prices subject to change without notice